ABOUT MY MOM:

This Is Mom

Her name: _____

How I call her _____

Her age: _____

She is _____ at work

MOM'S FAVORITE:

Food _____

Animal _____

Activity _____

Color _____

Flower _____

TOP 5

Great things about my mother

1. ....

2. ....

3. ....

4. ....

5. ....

Happiness is

MOTHER

and ME

Time

Our favorite thing to do together is

....

....

Mom And Me Drawing

I love hearing stories about

....

....

I love you because you tell me I am

....

....

I love it when we play

....

....

I love the way you give the best advice when

....

....

Draw Mom's favorite animal

I love you because
when I feel sick, you always

....

....

COLOR

I love you because you make the best

....

....

COLOR

BEST MOM EVER

I love that you taught me

....

....

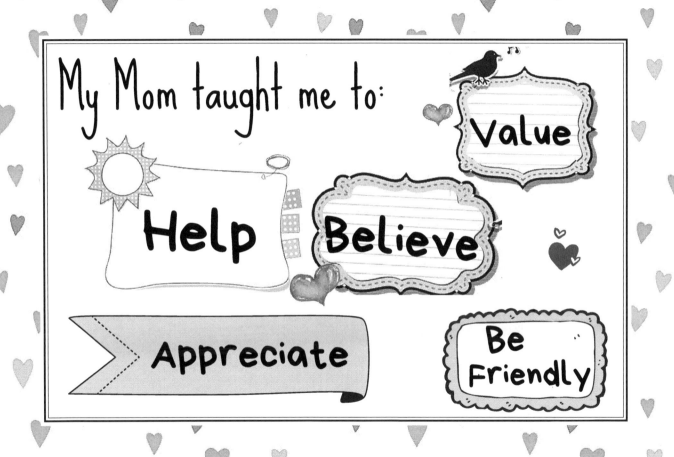

You are so funny when

....

....

This is Mom in three words:

I would like to learn more about

....

....

I was very proud when you

....

....

I tell my friends you are super
awesome because

....

....

I love you because
you build me up when you say

....

....

You deserve the

....

....

Award

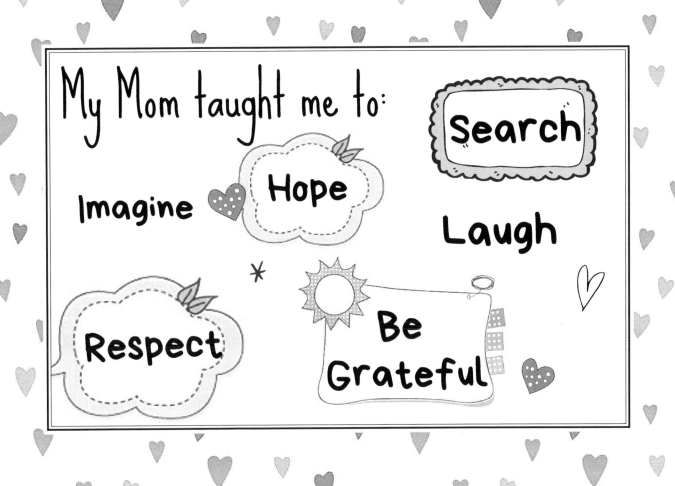

I will always cherish that day when

....

....

A picture of us:

I love you because you can

....

....

faster than anyone

Mom, you are my sunshine

I love you because
you are the best

....

....

I love you because you can fix

....

....

Draw a picture for your mom

I love you because
you make the yummiest

....

....

My favorite place to go with you is

....

....

Mom, you make the good
moments better and the
*
hard ones easier

I feel most loved when you

....

....

I would definitely like to do this

with you again

If you were a color, you'd be

....

....

Draw Mom's favorite flower

The most amazing thing we have done together is

....

....

I know you are the happiest when

....

....

This is Mom

By Me

I love the way you cheer when I

....

....

This is Me

By Me

My favorite thing to do together is

....

....

The funniest picture of Mom and Me

Together we make the absolute best

....

....

TEAM

Draw as many hearts as you can and color them

If you were a holiday, you'd be

....

....

I Love You,
Mom.
You Are
The Best

I know you love me because

....

....

I love that I got from you

....

....

"I love you more than all the frosting on a cupcake, Mom!"

The most important
thing I learned from you is

....

....

I am really grateful for

....

....

"Every day is special when I get to spend it with my mom."

You are the best
mom ever because

....

....

Want FREEBIES?

Email Us At:

larasvows@gmail.com

Title the email "What I Love About Mom For Kids"
and let us know that you purchased our book.

_____

THANKS FOR YOUR AMAZING SUPPORT!

>>>>>>>>>>>>>>>>>>>>>>>>>>>>>>>>>

For Enquiries and Customer Service
email us at:

larasvows@gmail.com

We don't exist without you. A brief review could help us a lot. Please leave your feedback about this book.

SCAN THE OR CODE BELLOW

>>>>>>>>>>>>>>>>>>>>>>>>>>>>>>>>>

THANKS FOR YOUR AMAZING SUPPORT!

Made in United States
Orlando, FL
09 June 2024